Ballistics Report

Also by Henry Rifle

✦ *Shooting Gallery*
✦ *Bullet Train*
✦ *A Bullet West*
✦ *The Henry Rifle Diet: It's Not Just for Swingers!*

To learn more about the late Henry Rifle, visit *www.henry-rifle.blogspot.com*

Ballistics Report

Henry Rifle

A Temporary POV Production

Produced by Flat Sole Studio,
398 Goodrich Avenue, St. Paul, MN 55102
www.flatsolestudio.com

Copyright © 2011 Dan Hendrickson

All rights reserved. No part of this publication
may be reproduced in whole or in part
without written permission of the publisher.

Library of Congress Cataloging-in-Publication Data
Rifle, Henry.
   Ballistics Report / by Henry Rifle.
   p. cm.
   Poems.
   ISBN 978-1-938237-23-2 (paperback)
   ISBN 978-0-9818279-9-5 (pbk. : alk. paper)
   ISBN 978-0-9818279-8-8 (ebk. : alk. paper)
   I. Title.
PS3618.I39375B35 2011
811'.6—dc22   2010040188

Photo Credits
Amy Hendrickson, cover, backcover, 27, 82–83
Francine Corcoran, 12
Shutterstock, cover and photo effects

Book and Cover Design
Flat Sole Studio

To Yoshimi

"First I was a poet. Then I became an outlaw.
Or was it the other way around? I can never keep it all straight."
— American poet (and outlaw) Henry Rifle

"The sky is a place for clouds to hang out; a stream is a graveyard for trout."
— Ancient Aztec saying.

Henry Rifle was an American poet, who, for a brief time in the early part of this century (21st), bestrode the stage like a minor colossus . . . before ultimately fading like the echo of a gunshot into the dullish roar of history. Not long afterwards, his travels took him out to Hollywood, and then on to old Mexico, where he met a somewhat untimely demise.

What follows is an informal record of what might possibly have happened next.

"The American poet Henry Rifle is dead STOP Send money STOP"
　　— Transcript of a telegraph sent early on the morning of Oct. 8, 2001.

Tumble Down Suite

The Crime in Question

    There's not much to it, really.
    I thought it was the perfect crime.
    Nobody got hurt
    or even threatened,
    and I wound up with a whole mess
    of fresh pesos.
    The Mexican authorities, simply put,
    disagreed with me.
    Long story short,
    we didn't see eye to eye
    on that particular topic.
    But the great thing was,
    we sat down and we
    hashed out our differences.
    That's the important thing.
    At the end of the day,
    that's
    what matters most.

BALLISTICS REPORT

SUBJECT:	Human
CLASSIFICATION:	American Poet
STATUS:	Deceased
CAUSE OF DEATH:	Bullet Overdose
ALIASES (known):	Dan Hendrickson, Danny Ramada, Stan Bernadino
ALIASES (previously unknown):	Johnny Canolli, Chet December, Skip Poughkeepsie
THROWS:	Right-handed

PERSONAL EFFECTS:
- One pair dark sunglasses
- One tie (bulletproof)
- One shirt (wrinkled)
- One pair of pants (unpressed)
- One pair of underwear (w/hearts)
- One pair of shoes (brown)
- No belt
- One pair of socks
- One rabbit's foot
- One ticket to 'La Boheme' (it's an op-er-a)
- Several unaddressed IOU's

"Is there room enough for two / if I ain't got a point of view?"
— Bash and Pop, "Never Aim to Please"

"*What are we but pipes for dreams…kegs for ammunition.*"
— From an unsent letter discovered in Henry Rifle's papers, all of which have since been recycled.

D.O.A.
(a poem joined in progress)

> . . . and they'll
> laugh about
> the way
> you twitched
> when you left
> this
> little world.

Transition Glasses

> There's a ghost in my shoes
> and he's wearing
> my pants.
> A part of me can't help
> but be curious
> about that.

It's Always What You Thought
(but never what you think)

    It wasn't at all
    the way I expected
    to go out.
    I always thought
    they'd find me
    floating face-down
    in a think tank.
    Or that I'd die
    in a massive
    yogurt explosion.
    But not like this.
    Never in a billion years
    like this.
    I guess it goes
    to show you,
    life is chockfull of surprises.
    Why, then,
    should death
    be any different?

June Panic

While I stood there patiently
waiting for the guns to sound,
I thought back to a time when
I checked into a Fargo hotel
on a lovely spring day.
When I asked the front desk guy
where I might go to enjoy the weather,
he gestured down a hallway and said,
'Might I suggest our courtyard?'
I thanked him, grabbed my key card,
picked up my bag
and started off towards my room,
when I heard him add quietly, *'of doom.'*
Whirling around, I said,
'I beg your pardon?'
He shook his head and said
that he hadn't said anything.
But when I turned around again,
I could hear him behind me,
chuckling evilly.

Mona Lisa

When I faced that firing squad,
I wasn't smiling because I was
wearing a bulletproof tie.
I was smiling simply
because I remembered
I had some dry cleaning
to pick up.
The thought of my pants
hanging there in the dock
for all eternity,
that debt forever going unpaid . . .
I guess you could say it
really struck a chord — no pun intended.
The Man ran the score up on me
for a great many years,
so to get a point back like that,
right at the buzzer . . .
it felt really, really good.

The Mudd Club

There was a time
when I thought
death was pretty darned glamorous.
Now I've come to realize
that when they're done
with you,
they simply toss you
in a box
and throw you in a hole.
Nothing
too glamorous
about that.

Final Inventory

There isn't a lot
to count up.
About all I really
left behind
was a sink full
of broken glass
and a bathtub
full of gin.

Which I know
some might say
is sad.
But I had some
big plans
— for that gin.

I really did.

Who Are You? (doot-doot-doot-doot)

I spent some time in
The City of Angels before
closing the show down in Mexico.
My last night in town I ran into yet another
sad case down on Sunset Boulevard.
It was nighttime, the stars were snug in bed.
I hitched up my worn jacket collar
and shuffled wearily up to the crime scene,
sipping on a stale cup of joe.
'What do we got, Lieu?' I asked.
Staring down at the body, the lieutenant said, *'Male victim, early 30's. Cause of death: blunt force trauma to the head.'*
I shook my head and stared out to sea.
I couldn't see it from where I was standing,
but I knew it was out there somewhere.
'75 degrees in the shade,' I said,
each word layered in jade,
'and this town just keeps getting colder.'
He nodded grimly, then looked over
in my direction.
'Hey, who the hell are you?' he demanded.
With that, I tossed my coffee cup aside
and sprinted off into the night.

A Lyrical Ghost w/a Tangible Dream

Some of my happiest days in L.A.
were my days with my 2nd band,
West of Seven.
Though we only lasted
through three rehearsals
and one half of a live show
before breaking up acrimoniously,
I like to think we were something
of a seminal band.
Seminal.
That's a word I never knew how
to pronounce.
Was it sem-in-al or *seem*-in-al?
Either way, there was plenty of that
going on, believe me, you.

What I Learned on My Summer Vacation

The first thing you learn
in Hollywood?
Keep the talent hydrated.
It's a well-documented fact that
simply to survive
famous people need
three times as much water as
the average human being.
Good water, too.
Not that rustwater you favor.
So if you can't even do that much,
you're just wasting your time.
You might as well go back
home at that point,
all the way back to Sheboygan, WI.
In fact, why
don't you leave right now?
Buy yourself a one-way ticket
and get on the bus tonight.
Make the trip all the way
back across country,
and give your Aunt (\ *'ant*\) Petunia
a big old hug when
you get back home.
There's at least a chance
she misses you.

Bad Reputation

People always thought
I was this bad guy
because I wanted to
smash everything
and burn what was left.
But I had a heart of gold,
I swear!

"A butterfly means nothing to a trout."
— Jacques Cousteau

Welcome to the Boomtown

The day they shot me down
was a fine winter day,
I have to say.
All things considered.
Winter in that part of Mexico
was like summer in most other places.
There was a nice breeze blowing
across the plaza
and the sun felt warm on my face
in contrast
to the cold brick at my back.
Everything was quiet
and still,
and just before
the crisp reports of guns
and muffled booms
echoed out across the valley,
a simple butterfly landed on my cheek.
It probably wasn't a butterfly.
More likely it was an old, greasy
tamale wrapper,
but it made me happy to think
that it might have been a butterfly.
Like a small sign from some other place
that things somehow still might be alright.
If nothing else, it would have been
one final kiss
of color
before everything
faded to black.

Maybe It's a Good Thing, Maybe It's . . .

Butterflies
have nothing
left
to dream about.

Members Only

When I was alive,
I did most of
my Official Drinking down
at the Club Lepidoptera.
It's a private club,
a long ways off
the beaten path.
Don't bother
looking for it.
You'll never find it.

The More Things Change

I'm not really sure how I'll like
being dead.
I was never very good
at dealing with change.
When I was alive, people
would tell me all the time
that I needed to learn to embrace
change.
I would reply by shouting,
'YOU need to learn to embrace change!'
Then I'd start to cry and run away.
It's funny, I never thought
I'd miss those days,
but I'm thinking now
I might.

I'm Not There, Either

In a way, the end
comes as something of a relief.
At least now I don't have
to worry about
getting whacked anymore.
I used to worry about that
all the time.
In fact, there were times
when I was home alone
where I would hide for hours,
just on the off-chance
some mob goon would
come along and try to
whack me.
That way, he'd take a quick
look around my apartment and
assume I'd stepped out.
Meanwhile, I'd be
sprawled out
behind the couch,
trying not to giggle.

Code of Conduct

What I hated more
than anything about this
place was how,
when
you were sitting
in a fancy restaurant
having dinner by yourself,
your therapist would
march up to your table,
point at you and shout,
for all the other diners to hear,
'HE'S *completely insane!!*'
That's not professional.
I don't care what
anyone says.

My Own Private View

If I get to be a ghost
on a long-term basis —
and I think I have a case —
you won't ever find me
up in a tree.
If you ask me,
ghosts have no business
up in trees.
Unless
they're ghost birds
— or ghost monkeys.
That I could see.

A Serious Artist

A lot of people said
I wasn't a serious artist.
That's not true.
I was an extremely serious artist.
There were years I'd go months
without smiling.
Top that, Bob DeNiro!
Top that, Sean Penn!
Lousy amateurs.

A Little Grist for the Mill

Something you may not
have known about me?
I did all of my writing
on an old Smith-Corona typewriter.
It's true.
Unfortunately, my machine was a little
run-down.
It required a new ribbon after every five keystrokes.
Also, the only keys that still worked were
q, r, l, u and z, which made it a little tricky
to navigate sometimes.
But I was old school.
A real stickler,
if you will.

A Henry Rifle Original Poem (unedited)

Rluqs lrz rqu
Quzkuzq lrz qluz
Q ruzql lrzu q rlu
Zl qluzlr quz luu.

"You can put a saddle on the moon, but that don't make it a horse."
　　　— Henry Rifle

Night and Day

Mercutio's Blues

It appears the earth was cast
by a thoughtful potter.
The moon, by a talented provincial
who never quite broke free of their orbit.
When the moon debuted,
it was almost certainly
panned universally.
'Unaccomplished,' I'm sure,
was a common review.
Other skeptics probably derided
the satellite's
decided lack of artifice
– and criticized it's orbit.
For centuries, it's possible scarcely anyone
looked up to it at all.
Then, eventually, perhaps
it was the bohemians who rediscovered it.
Songs were composed, paintings
created, ripe poetry harvested
beneath its placid beams.
And, lo, over the course
of many, many centuries,
that moon
slowly became the focus
of countless hopes and dreams.
It hangs there gracefully yet today,
a glowing reminder that
yesterday's disasters
sometimes prove to be
tomorrow's masterpieces.

Veronica Mars (aka Good Neighbor)

The moon
had a lady friend
over last evening.
AND she spent the night!
Ooh la la!

Moon Patrol

If someone told me
a rocket had been
stolen,
the first place
I always looked
was the moon.
Nine times
out of ten,
I'd get that
rocket back for them.
And that 10th time?
That, my good friends,
is precisely
what rocket insurance
was for.

Return to Sender

The sun is a lot like a mail carrier,
only instead of bringing fresh mail
each day
she brings fresh
UV's and Vitamin D.
However, unlike a mailman,
you can't throw an empty
beer can at her
if she's late delivering your sunshine
three days in a row.
I mean, you can,
but you probably
won't hit her.
Still, I don't recommend
or condone throwing
anything at Postmen or Postwomen.
That's a Federal Offense, chum.
And if you don't believe me,
you can ask my Cousin Roy.
He'll tell you.
Only you can't speak to him
directly.
You'll have to write him
in care of Leavenworth Prison.
The mail service is awfully slow there,
but — and you can take my word for this —
he will get back to you.

Simple Physics

I read somewhere
that the moon is moving
slowly away from the earth.
Now the earth knows
how I always felt at parties.
How does it feel, Earth?
It doesn't feel good, does it?
Does it?!
No, it doesn't.

Calling It Just Like I See It

The sun is
a gaseous tramp
who gives her love away
to every single person she meets,
but I don't hear anyone saying
nasty things about her
when her back is turned.

No-good hypocrites.

Solstice

I'll never forget the summer
I owed my astronaut friend money.
He'd call me every day and tell
me there was
no place — no place —
in the whole universe I could hide.
That was
the worst summer of my life.

Glare

The sun's
a fiery bride
who's
graciously agreed
to marry
us all,
despite
her initial
misgivings.

The Sun Shines Free of All Things

You have nothing to lose
by giving your love away.
You can always
make more.

Reverse Engineering

Love's the answer,
stuff's the clues
and we're
the mysteries.

The 2nd Best Piece of Advice I Could Ever Give You

Be like the sun.
Radiate
good things.

Turntable

So you say the sky
is blue.
Maybe
you're depressed.

Palette Cleanser

Heaven's the place
where even the sky
runs out of blue
and has to find
another color.

The Best Piece of Advice I Could Ever Give You

Always
be where you are
when you are.
Traveling through time
is a sin.

The Bottom Line

We're all just
blinking satellites
trying
to get home.

Zen Philosophy

Spirit Guide

One very low day at
lunchtime
I asked the Zen Master,
'What could be sadder than cold soup?'
He said, *'Cornmeal baked in the rain.'*
I took that
with a pinch of pepper
and a grain of salt.
Then later, while eating lunch
on a far more buoyant day,
I inquired of him,
*'What could be more hopeful
than fresh bread?'*
He said simply, *'Cornmeal shared
before dawn.'*

I said, *'You're really hung up
on the cornmeal, aren't you?'*

Zen Comb-over

When you stop
looking
for the answers,
the answers
come looking
for you.

Unless they're
tied up
or have
better
things to do.

Logic Need Not Apply

I never had
a literary agent.
If I had
had
a literary agent,
you could have
picked up the phone and called her.
She would have told you
the exact same thing.

The Silence Is Complete

There was once a great zen monk named Basho.
Basho had an apprentice who showed promise,
but was very headstrong.
One night at dinner, Basho noticed
his apprentice hadn't eaten his dessert.
'You should eat your dessert,' said Basho.
'Will the bees not always make honey?' replied his apprentice
cavalierly, before departing from the dining hall early.
Basho frowned.

A short time later, Basho and his apprentice
were walking in the forest,
when a bear came upon them
and began to attack the apprentice.
'Master, help me!' the apprentice screamed.
Basho replied simply, *'I told you
you should have eaten your dessert!'*
The apprentice was shamed.
He bowed his head (as the bear mauled him) and said,
'My pain is the root, my love is the flower.'

'And your awareness is the vase in which it rests,'
said the Master,
thoughtfully completing the sentence.
Then he reached into his robe
and tossed the rest of the apprentice's dessert
to the bear. The bear released the apprentice
and eagerly devoured the sweet remnants.
The Master and Apprentice turned and started back
towards the monastery without a word between them.
There was nothing left to say.

Tyrants, Jesters and Slings

This world
has ground
the philosophers
to dust.
All that's left now
are tyrants,
jesters
and slings.

R.I.P.

Philosophers wore
logical socks
and inherently
practical shoes.

Resilient

Mountains are
stone poets,
philosophers
whose views
are constantly
being re-shaped.

Anchors Away

Philosophers were
the tarnished anchors
on the ocean floor
which kept
the ships from smashing
in a storm.

Bouncing Slowly into Focus

Yesterday's a thief,
tomorrow's
a poet,
today's
a tramp —
oline!

Universal Prescription

The world
is a gritty pill
we all
have to swallow.
My advice
to you?
Drink lots of water.
It goes down
a little smoother.

Poems Here on Earth

Wake-up Call

    People on TV
    were always talking
    about the car
    of my dreams.
    I rarely dreamt
    about cars.

Rest of the Story

    What I dreamt about
    was a world
    where people were free,
    finally free,
    of boxes.
    And a world where
    the only things
    in foxholes
    were foxes.

Color Bars

I think people
should say
what they want
and think
what they will —
within reason
and applicable
statutes.

This
is only
a test.

Most Dreams Are Roundtrip

I was lying in bed
one morning
when I heard
a plane overhead.
I let my head
scroll across the pillow
so I could see the alarm clock.
It read: 7:47.
I thought about that
for a little bit,
then glanced away
and thought about it
a little more.
When I looked
back at the clock again,
it was 7:48
and the drone of the plane
was gone.
I wonder to this very day,
was it all a dream?

Color Full

Everyone's
a bucket
of fun
waiting
to be spilled.

Comparing Notes

Have you ever thought
somebody was your friend,
only to realize later maybe
they *weren't* your friend?
Only to go back over your
notes at some point later in time
and realize perhaps they WERE
your friend after all?
And then, after giving it
some more thought — and
doing some research
on the Internet – come
to the subsequent conclusion that they were,
in all likelihood, NOT your friend?
But then woken up in traffic
sometime after that, even, and realized
that not only were they
your friend, they were also
your first cousin twice removed?
That never happened to me,
but it certainly sounds
like an intriguing scenario.
I'll grant you that
any day of the week.

The Funny Thing About Whistlin' Pete

The guy never whistled — ever.
None of us ever
heard him whistle,
not even once,
and *no one* remembers
how he got his nickname.
But, that's what we called him
and that's what he'll be called
every day for the rest of his life,
right up until the day that he dies.
It's kind of sad
when you think about it.
I tried not to.

You Know You Know

When I was a kid,
one of my very best friends
was a pirate.
Back then, my parents
refused to take
him sailing with us.
I lost touch with him
over the years, but
recently found out
he owns a radio station now.
And NO, it's not a
pirate radio station.
People can change,
you know.
Sheesh!
A guy shouldn't have
to go to JCPenney
just to get some slack(s).

Fairly Clear-cut

You don't have to
cut down a tree
to prove you're a lumberjack.
If you wear a flannel shirt
and carry an axe around
everywhere you go,
we're going to get the picture.
We're not stupid,
you know.

Ellis Island

My family got to America
sometime in 1905.
We would have been here earlier,
but my great-great grandpa had
an irrational fear of large women.
He got one look at
The Statue of Liberty
and didn't stop screaming
until they got him back to Norway.

All about the Benjamins

I used to always have this dream.
In that dream I'd wake up,
though I was still really asleep,
and just know
General George Washington
himself was outside chopping
down my apple tree.
I'd get dressed and go
out back, and sure enough,
he'd be there in the moonlight,
standing beside my felled apple tree,
resting his weight regally against his axe,
as though he had just crossed
the Delaware on foot.
'Dammit, George,' I'd say,
*'why can't you leave
my damn apple tree alone?'*
He would turn to me
and he would say — in a voice
like Robert DeNiro in any one of the
47 mobster movies he's starred in —
*'You saw nutting — you hear me?
You saw nutting.'*
Then he would walk up to me,
stuff a crisp bank note
into the breast pocket of my
pajamas and give my cheek
a light slap.
I would look at him,
and then glance down skeptically
at the fresh one-dollar bill
jutting out of my pocket.
And I would wonder
why it couldn't ever
just once be
Benjamin Franklin
who chopped down
my dream apple tree.

"Abe Lincoln: fascinating fellow. Someone should write a book about him."
— Henry Rifle

Someone Who Got It

Allegedly, shortly after
Abe Lincoln was assassinated,
his young son Tad asked someone
if his father was in heaven.
Whomever he asked replied, *'Yes.'*
Upon hearing that, young Tad
seemed satisfied — pleased.
He said something to that effect
and then noted, *'This place wasn't
good for him.'*
And it was clear he wasn't simply talking
about the White House.
Upon reading this exchange
I wanted to ruffle the hair on that
kid's head.
Because it's clear to me that he
must have been a lot
like his dad: someone
who got it.
And there aren't
many people in this world
who get it.
Most of them who do
are either hanging silently
on staid museum walls
or sitting placidly on
marble horses deep in
the hearts of city parks,
forever frozen in granite.
And that's a real pity,
of course,
but there it is.
And there you
have it.

"The man who wears lemon shoes walks a bitter path."
  — Socrates

Songs about Lemons

Absurdist Fare

You can put
a lemon
in shoes, but
first
you have
to slice
it in half.
Is it worth
all that extra effort?
You tell me,
Mr. Grassy Knoll.
You tell me,
Mr. Lemon-in-your-shoes!

Lemon Perspective

My only real regret is that
I never got to finish writing
my book on greed and cynicism.
Of course, I was only writing it
for the money.
And, frankly, I don't know why
I even bothered.
No one probably would have
bought it anyway.

"Yesterday's a lime, tomorrow's a tangerine, today's a mashed potato on the vine."
— Old Yiddish saying.

When Life Hands You Lemon Sharks

The only things clinically proven
to repel Lemon Sharks
are tangerines.
Oh, you can try
clementines.
That is, if you're the type
of person who enjoys
being mauled
by ravenous Lemon Sharks.
But if you're serious
about this, I'd suggest
a trip to your local grocer
before you get into
the water.
Or, who knows?
Maybe you're the sort
who enjoys being
gnawed on
by Lemon Sharks.
Maybe that's your thing.
Who am I to judge?
We all
have our things . . .

Cookbook

Give a man a fish
and you feed him
for a day.
Teach a man to fish
and you feed him
for a lifetime.
And, finally,
give a lemon a chicken
and dinner
is served.

"Shakespeare was a poet. Kafka was a lemon thief."
— Old Minsk proverb

Shopping Trip

I used to hate going
to the grocery store
in my neighborhood.
The manager there
used to love
to torment me.
Every time I walked into
the place, he'd smile and turn
to his flunkies, who never seemed
to have anything else to do
but stand around
and wait for me to do my shopping.
'Well, looky-looky here,' he'd say,
in this real loud voice,
'it's old Lemon-dome!'
I would just pick up a shopping basket,
put my citrusesque head down
and try
to ignore his gibes.
*'What are you shopping for
today, Lemon-dome?'* he'd ask in an acid tone,
tailing me and playing to the crowd.
*'A couple of lemons to go with your
BIG LEMON DOME?'*
To this very day
I don't know why
I did all of my shopping there.
There was a Safeway
not two blocks up the road.

Clunker

I hate to admit it,
but the truth of it is
I was a real lemon in bed.
In fact, I was so bad,
some people went so far
as to ask
for their money back
when it was all over.
I never argued, not once.
I just wrote
the check.
Even if they had just paid me
in cash.
Normally that wasn't
a problem.
But, occasionally, there
were some issues with
accounting errors and what not
down at the bank,
which led to hard feelings and overdraft fees.
Yeah, I don't know what it was,
but they could never quite seem
to get their act together.
Down there
at the bank.

Aesthetically Speaking

No one wants
to go through
life
with a lemon
in their chest.
Luckily, if that's
your prognosis,
there is a known cure.
All you really
need to do
is take the time
to find
some sugar
and a glass,
then ask
someone to
give you
a squeeze.
Then chill.
Or serve over ice.

Pining for the Good Old Days
Sometimes I wish
I would have lived
back in the good old days.
Back when a quarter
lasted for two weeks and
lemons still grew on trees.
If I had, I'd have taken me a quarter
and bought me TWO lemon trees.
Can you say *'all the lemonade you can drink?'*

Yeah, I thought you could.
Way to go, slugger.
Gold star for you.

Flashback Poem
(edges poking through)

I feel like
an old burlap sack
filled
with broken glass.

Who needs a hug?

Memory Circuit

A long time ago, back
when I was most likely depressed
enough to be
hooked up to a machine,
I took a few courses at
the local university.
One of them was an acting class.
Now I was no Jack Lemmon, but I did
learn a few things in that class.
What I remember most about it
was the night a few of us wannabe actors
volunteered to be ushers
for a student production of some kind.
Basically, we collected tickets from people
and helped them to their seats.
It was a pretty simple gig, and I
was surprised to find
I enjoyed it thoroughly,
even though it didn't pay a thing.
In fact, though I was almost entirely
miserable then, I was happy that one night.
And I didn't stick around for the show,
though I could have, for free.
Still, I learned a good lesson,
and the lesson I learned was that
even if I couldn't
enjoy the show in the least,
I could still help other people
find their seats.

"The real worry is whether markets, and the machines that increasingly drive them, will do irrational things."
 — From the June 7, 2010 issue of *Newsweek*.

The Industrial Revolution

After All

    It occurred to me
    awhile back
    that we're all —
    sort of —
    in this together.
    We're all strapped
    to the same rack,
    stuck in the same traffic.
    We all breathe
    the same
    poisons and we're all
    being worked mercilessly
    by the same sad hustle.
    Now there may or
    there may not be a Santa Claus,
    West Virginia,
    but lately I've begun to think
    that little cricket was right:
    It really *is*
    a small world.

Supernovocaine

It's a painless
little world
we live on.
Hardly anyone feels
a thing.

"My artificial tears aren't enough. Is there something more?"
         — from a magazine advertisement for Restasis

Downstream

Tears are trickles
of hope
in this place.
Proof
that someone
yet feels.

Nouns

In the end,
only things
can make us happy.
Things like waterfalls
and laser beams.
You know it's true.
Admitting it
doesn't make you
a bad person.
Not necessarily.

Smoke Finds the Ceiling; Ash Finds the Floor

Water's
always
falling.
You never
see it
rise,
except
as
steam.

"... but this machine can only swallow money..."
— R.E.M., 'The Sidewinder Sleeps Tonight.'

Post Road

I read a short story when I was young.
It was set back in the olden days,
the 1950's, maybe,
and it was about a guy who
was hired to dig post holes;
literally, he dug holes for posts,
and he was on a crew of guys
who did that day in and day out,
generally in the middle of nowhere.
One of the guys he worked with
was really good at his job.
So good, in fact, he would dig
out ahead of the crew a little
more each day until one day
he finally disappeared out over the horizon.
The story ended with the narrator
looking up at the crater-pocked moon
sometime later,
and the subtle insinuation was
that the lost digger
had perhaps gotten out so far ahead
of the crew, he had created those holes too.
I still think about that story,
and the character who went machine.
That can be tempting.
This world sometimes
all but drives us to do it,
chipping away at our humanity,
stripping us of our dignity . . .
leaving us cold and remote.

But if you find yourself on that path
you must turn back.
You. Must.
Man is not machine
and should never
strive to be.

"The heart is the soul's ashtray."
— Danish maxim.

Typing Pool

Dancing with a broken heart
is like trying to type
with broken fingers.
The pay is $5 an hour.
You start Tuesday.

Every Day's Your Birthday

They're slicing up
this thoughtful
cake
and lining up
for pieces!

The Teflon Approach

More than anything else,
I hated being labeled.
Because as soon as someone
says you're this, then more
often than not,
you can't be that.
And maybe I really wanted
to be that.
Maybe I wanted it more than
anything in the whole world.
It's possible.
You don't know.
I'm not a machine.
I get
to have secrets.

August, 1913

I have no desire
to go back in time, ever.
But if I had the chance
to go back just once,
I'd go back to 1913,
the year Henry Ford
turned us all into machines.
I think I'd try to have
a little fun
as long as I was there.
I'd walk up to Old Henry
and say, *'Hello-Henry,*
my-name-is-Henry-too.
Watch-me-do-my-futuristic-
dance.'
Then I'd do the robot dance.
Or perhaps The Safety Dance.
Whichever one would blow
his primitive 20th-century brain
into a deeper orbit

Bonus Poem

My time machine broke.
Now I'm stuck
with these lunkheads
in the 21st century.
Dear Lord in Heaven,
do I need a drink.

Gear Daddies

> The Machine
> runs itself now.
> All we are is the grease
> that keeps it
> running smooth
> and
> the stuff
> that gets caught
> in the gears.

Life in Century 21

> Mine was a fairly
> modern existence,
> I suppose.
> I sometimes fell asleep
> wanting to cry
> and often
> woke up screaming.

So Close and Yet So Far

> I never lived long enough
> to get to the point in time where
> you could take your thoughts
> and download them onto a CD.
> If I had, I would have
> done just that, and then
> run a magnet back and forth
> across that CD a few times
> before uploading those thoughts
> back into my brain
> via a secure link.
> Just to see what that
> was all about.

Self-assessment 24

> I was an economic prisoner,
> same as any other.
> There was nothing
> special about me.

True Patriot

Some people might choose
to question
my patriotism
posthumously,
a charge I would find
patently absurd.
I was very patriotic.
I was so patriotic, in fact,
I slept with my hand on my chest,
just in case I happened to mutter
the Pledge of Allegiance
in my sleep.
In fact, if a person
were to meet me and then
meet Ben Franklin,
they'd walk away thinking,
*'My God! Ben Franklin
is a frickin' commie!'*
And I'd just stand there smiling,
waving my little flag and chanting quietly,
'U-S-A. U-S-A.'

Self-assessment 55

Mine was just
another voice
lost
in the American Scream.

The West Never Really Gets Old

In America,
guns are expensive
but the bullets are free.
If'n you know
what I mean.

Henry Rifle

Progress

A lot of people
say we haven't made
as much progress
as maybe we should
have — as human beings.
I'd dispute that.
Do you realize
there's nowhere
on this world you can go now,
absolutely nowhere,
where they can't
blow you to smithereens?
Nowhere!
So don't tell me
that's not progress, Comrades.
I don't want
to hear it!

Zen Snipers

Zen snipers
never fire a shot.
They are at one
with their targets.

The Lesson of Sundance

Sometimes you have
to jump
off the rocks
and hope
you hit water.

Things No One Ever Said in Real Time

— Many a heart has been swayed by the ocean.

— It's never too early to rain and never too late to shine.

— Cardboard philosophers hate rain.

— Sometimes it takes a mystery to solve a clue.

— The spider may die, but the web still catches.

— Being kind is a small investment that pays nice dividends.

— A thoughtful rain might never fall.

— Life isn't all porcini mushrooms and blackberry jam.

— We all shift and stand in the same permutating sands of inevitability.

— The heart is a dark target.

— It's tough to feast on the bones of indecision.

— When you point out another's flaws, you expose one of your own.

— Stars are clumsy things.

— Flowers keep the hills standing and hills give flowers a place to stand.

— Everyone bleeds in a cutthroat society.

— Sailors are generally as heartless as the oceans they sail upon.

— Real stars shine for free.

— If you want to defy gravity, all you have to do is smile.

— Robots have feelings too.

— Everything sinks in a bottom line world.

— A country that lets attack dogs shape its policy runs the risk of becoming a junkyard.

Henry Rifle

— The only thing that can stop a waffle train is syrup.
— Whales are ambassadors of the ocean, champions of the deep.
— You can't bottle strange, but you can put a cork in it.
— Evolution scares none so much as those who believe themselves incapable of it.
— That which can be emptied can often be refilled
— The world is a swirling mass of contradictions orbiting a steady source of love.
— Life's a static poem in need of constant tuning.
— Ideas queue in space and patiently wait for receivers.
— The heart is a flexible document.
— In wild fields you'll find more life than in fields planted right.
— The rational trout rarely ends up as dinner.
— Debts go unpaid from generation to generation, and in that fashion are repaid.
— As your capacity for darkness grows, so does your capacity for light.
— A world free of philosophy is bound to be a prison.
— Sometimes it takes a lion to tame a grizzly bear.
— The human heart is a subduction zone.
— The sun is a shining card in the cold deck of the night.
— We shoot up only so tall, then we have to grow roots.
— The heart is a rucksack for dreams.
— It takes a long pencil to erase that which is written in the stars.

The cover photo of Henry Rifle's legendary lost volume of poetry, "Henry Rifle Slept Naked Here".*

* This book is exceptionally rare. Finding a copy in any condition is akin to finding a pristine Gutenberg Bible with a mint condition Honus Wagner baseball card tucked inside — signed by J.D. Salinger.

Songs About Whales

Gunwale

    I always considered myself
    an introspective whale.
    I took in sounds
    and did my best
    to make sense of them.

Pea in a Pod

    If I
    were a whale
    I'd undoubtedly
    be gray.
    Or, perhaps, blue.
    What's more,
    I'm fairly sure
    I'd blur
    the lines
    between the two.

    In fact,
    there were times
    — back when I was alive —
    when, while strolling
    down the beach in a
    crisp business suit,
    intuitive whales
    would often mistake me
    for one
    of their own.

Civil Wear

I liked to dress up
when I visited the beach.
I thought it sent a real message
to both the shallow
and the deep.

Ampersand

Even the most rational
whales
can easily imagine
the bitter taste of sand.
The relentless drying winds
onshore,
the heaviness
of land.

Depth Finder

I was only as crazy
as I needed to be
to make it
through
a given day.
But I
could
go deeper
if conditions
required it.

Killer whales
had nothin'
on me.

Poof, Magic — Gone

I had this cousin.
He was a real 'go with the flow'
kind of fellow.
We were swimming in the river
once, long ago, when a gentle
current
carried him slowly downstream,
around the bend
and out of sight.
I never heard
from him again.

Feeding Frenzy

Life isn't all
fun and games
and
wet kisses.
Sometimes
it's rain
and bronchitis.
Still, whether
fish, man or
woman,
life's all about
dodging hooks.
It's a shame
the bait
is so tasty.

Oysters

What I used to like to do
was ask my friends
about their sex lives.
Quite often, they were
willing to provide
some pretty choice tidbits.
Up until the point I took out a pen
and paper and began
to jot down notes.
Then they tended to clam up.
I never understood why.

It's all good.

Readers Digest

This mechanized world
has made us
numb
unfeeling things,
like hollow shells buried deep
in cold, damp sand.
All of us working
slowly on
our own bits of
internal shrapnel.
Clutter stuck
inside of us,
the shards
we can't
process.

Our jobs, then,
are to find ways
to reach out
in the dark
and reconnect,
to discover
means of making pearls
from the grit
within
our chests.

Fluid Dynamics

If I were a wave,
I'd slosh
against shore.
No crashing,
no histrionics.

Pearls in Black Sand

The stars
in the sky
are a scattered mess.
Still,
each one of them
shines.

Like and Like

Like whales,
we struggle
in the deep,
but even
moreso
in the shallows.

"Early morning drinking tea / a slice of whole wheat."
— Bash and Pop, "Loose Ends"

Breakfast Poems

Blowing Hickory Smoke

Some people wanted
to get rich fast.
Not me.
I wanted to get rich
slow.
Yessiree,
I wanted to
savor it.
Like bacon.

Combo Platter

Other than breakfast
there wasn't much
I found all that interesting
in this world.
In fact, sometimes I think
if it hadn't been for corn mazes
and volcanoes,
I might very well have gone insane.

Links

The American meat-grinder
makes sausage of us all.
To be clear, though,
you could say the same thing
about any country.
If you lived in Holland, you
could say the Dutch meat-grinder
makes sausage of us all.
If you lived in Taiwan,
you could say the Taiwanese meat-grinder
makes sausage of us all.
Or, if you lived in Vienna, you could say
the Viennese meat-grinder
makes sausage of us all.
Which seems somehow appropriate.

Smokehouse

    Everybody down here
    suffers — from something.
    The great thing about this place
    is that there's a ready remedy waiting
    for everyone.
    What's more, you don't have
    to go looking for it.
    It's coming for you
    even as I type this very sentence,
    if it hasn't locked in
    on your position already.
    And I don't care what
    it is that afflicts you:
    pride, spite,
    hate, envy,
    bitterness,
    jealousy or greed,
    I promise . . .
    this world
    will cure you.

    Like bacon.

Eggs and Folks

    Some break fast,
    some
    break slow.
    I liked mine
    over easy.

Two Dreams Per Day Came True

Some folks store their dreams
in empty coffee cans.
Who am I to say
they're wrong?
I drank mine by the cup.

Dental Plan

Life kicks you in the teeth
until it likes the look
of your smile.
Then, to show you
it's not all bad,
it takes you out
for a huge breakfast
of steak and eggs.
And kicks you
again
when you don't
take a bite.
Life is short.
Don't forget
to floss.

We All Break the Same

I dreamt once that
I was an empty bottle
of syrup
and I was tossed out
into the recycle bin.
All of the other empty
bottles
were whiskey bottles
and they didn't like me
one bit.
They glared at me
and were all like,
'You f'n pussy,'
and saying lots of other
unpleasant things like that.
I woke up thinking,
'That's what I'll miss
about this place someday.
Everyone's so nice.'

Really Big

Tom Hanks sometimes
made cameos in my dreams.
The times he stopped by,
I'd always have coffee on the boil.
Cheap coffee, but still coffee,
so I'd offer him a cup — knowing
I had to — but also knowing I was
handing him a bland cup of joe.
The funny thing was, even though
he had to be miserable,
he never said a thing.
He just smiled and talked and
drank his coffee, and then never failed
to thank me on his way out the door.
Which goes to show you,
even in the dreams
of a nobody like me,
Tom Hanks is a heckuva nice fella.

Self-assessment 29

I often thought of myself
as being like peanut butter;
pleasant to have around,
but when it's gone
no one really misses it.
Just for kicks, I'd sometimes try to imagine
the world after my death.
I'd often picture a scene like this:
a guy going through his cupboards
and calling out, *'Hey, honey?*
What happened to the peanut butter?'
And his wife replying casually from the other room
— without looking up from her newspaper —
'He died alone, by the railroad tracks.'
The husband, digesting that calmly, says,
'Oh.
Do we have any jelly?'

Lost in Translation

My last night in Mexico
I was watching this great
movie on Telemundo.
I wasn't able to find out how
it ended, though, because it was late
and my translator wanted to go home.
I told him I would whip up a late night
breakfast if he could just stick around
but he smiled and said,
'I've had your cooking before, Senor.'
I couldn't argue with that logic.
After he left, I turned off the television
and debated making breakfast anyway.
But I was tired too, so I just climbed into bed
and tried to dream of bacon.

A Little More About My Cooking

The first time I asked my translator
to try my cooking and give me his
honest opinion, he took a bite,
looked off into the distance
and told me it tasted
like a barely-suppressed panic attack.
He added that he hoped he hadn't
offended me.
I told him I wasn't offended at all.
On the contrary, I told him he might
very well have a second career
waiting for him as a food critic.

A Little Seasoning

Back in college I had a roommate who
was studying to be a diplomat.
So what I would do was offer
to cook dinner, purposely
botch the recipe and serve him
meals I knew were largely inedible.
Then afterwards I would ask him
what he thought of it.
That might sound a bit cruel, I suppose,
but I was simply preparing him
for his future.

Make of It What You Will

I'm not sure if I'll miss poetry,
but maybe I will.
I don't know, but I do know that
not so long ago I dreamt
I was a retired waffle salesman
living out my days in Flapjack, Tennessee.
And I was sitting on a park bench
when someone came along
and asked me if I missed the waffle game.
I didn't reply.
What I did do, however,
was start to cry.
And my tears?
They were made out of 100% pure
maple syrup.

True story.
Make of it
what you will.

Dream Lab

How do I know it was 100% pure
maple syrup?
I collected a sample and brought
it over to the Dream Lab.
I slept in a little later than usual
to ensure I'd have enough time
to get the results back.
The staff at the Dream Lab,
they're a pretty efficient bunch.

Food Therapy

When you're
battered,
make pancakes

when you're
toasted
make tea

when you're
scrambled
make eggs

it's easy,
you see.

The End

Land of Libertine

    A lot of people seemed to place
    a lot
    of emphasis
    on being faithful in this world.
    That sounds terrific in theory,
    but in general practice, well,
    let's just say the whole
    concept's subjective.
    Because if being faithful meant
    you could only have one lover,
    then...why not one tire?
    Why not one shoe?
    I don't understand.
    I *thought*
    you were true.

Self-assessment 96

    Perhaps things would
    have turned out better
    if I had
    had a mentor of some kind.
    I thought I had a mentor once,
    but he turned out to be
    just some dork
    on a trampoline.
    How could I have
    been so deceived?!

Job Opening

Poets have to be
willing to hurl
themselves
recklessly into
hazy blue skies,
clouds thick and bland,
and discover
in flight
a
safe way
to land.

Job Description

A poet's job
is to stand in the cracks
and to try
to break
the thing.

Fame and Fortunes

About a week before
I bought it, I got my fortune
told one last time.
The fortune teller,
after a quick glance at my palm,
fell asleep for roughly 30 minutes.
I sat there quietly waiting for her.
When she awoke, she blinked
a couple of times and looked surprised
to find me still sitting there.
Then she said, *'You're going to be
a rock star. Oh, yeah. It just
came to me – in a vision.'*
I told her I didn't want to be
a rock star.
She asked me then
what I had wanted to be
when I grew up.
I told her I didn't remember.
She reached across the table, patted my
hand, and told me to hang on to
my dreams because
'they're all we really have in this world.'
I looked at her, then,
and began to laugh
hysterically.
Although
to the casual observer
it may have looked
as though
I was crying.

The Los Angeles River

We're all just drops in this river
which bleeds out to sea.
Remember my pants;
they deserved better than me.

Studio For Rent

The Beatles stopped touring
after a certain point because
they realized there were things
they could do in the studio
that they simply couldn't do
out on the road.
I reached that same conclusion myself.
I stopped doing poetry readings because
I realized there were things I could do
in my studio apartment
that I couldn't do onstage.
Like sit around in my underwear all day
and eat potato chips.
The Beatles were a band
far ahead of their time.
I was just a little bit behind.

Objective

One thing I won't miss?
Résumés.
Summing up your life in one page,
that was the best joke of all.
All anyone cared about is where you'd worked,
what you could do.
They never asked
about the best thing you'd ever done
— like freeing a monarch
dashing itself blue
against a dusty window inside
an old farm shed.
Not even
if that happened
to be true.

A Parting Gift

Though you will never, never,
never, never, NEVER EVER
find Club Lepidoptera,
if you should somehow trip across it –
and clear all the many preliminary barriers
and hurdles necessary to join the club –
here's the last thing you have to do to become
an official member in good standing.
When that day arrives and the barkeep
approaches you
and says, *'Excuse me, but have you seen the movie Cocoon?'*
What you need to do is look him
dead in the eye — I mean, dead —
and say,
'Seen it? Fucker, I've LIVED it!'
You did not hear that from me.

Role Model

I lived my life a very certain way.
I lived by a code.
When confronted with conflict,
I would ask myself,
'What would Robert Frost do?'
Then I would think,
'Wait a minute.
I don't know Robert Frost.
I don't know the first thing
about the guy!
I wouldn't know him if he
walked in here right now, punched me
in the teeth and lifted my wallet clean.'
From there,
I would just sort of . . . wing it.
To be honest,
it always surprised me
that a poet as esteemed
as Robert Frost
would act in such a manner.
You think you know someone..

Dear Hector Elizondo

You can live your whole life
and never quite say all you mean to say.
I know this because I always
meant to write Hector Elizondo to tell him
I had a cat which
reminded me quite a lot of him.
But I could never find
a way to say that.
What I mean when I say my cat
reminded me of Hector Elizondo is that
he was a bit . . . rough around the edges, deep-voiced,
and yet somehow very stately and elegant.
I tried to write Hector about this more than once,
but it's a nearly impossible letter to write.
Which is not to say I didn't try.

Dear Hector Elizondo,

I think you're a great actor, one of our very finest. I particularly enjoyed your work in 'Pretty Woman.' That part where you bailed Julia Roberts out of a tough jam is one of only seven parts in the movie that still make me cry each time I watch it. Anyway, I have this cat and . . .

Dear Hector Elizondo,

You won't believe this — and I know you'll think I'm crazy when I say this — but I have this cat and sometimes when the light hits him a certain way . . .

Dear Hector Elizondo,

Have you ever heard that thing that says people eventually start to look like their pets? I think that's a pile of rubbish, myself. But on a related note . . .

Oh, Hector Elizondo,
if you only knew
I once had a cat
who looked
very much like you.

Self-evaluation

Sometimes I think I should
have accomplished more
as a writer.
Then I think about Leo Tolstoy,
who wrote the classic novel
War and Peace.
And there's still war.
There's still peace.
I think I did alright.

Final Assessment

Was I a great man?
I don't know.
Was Socrates
a great man?
Was Aristotle
a great man?
Yes.
I was a great man.

Summation

It's tough to
warp the world
enough to fit
your bent perspective.
I did
the best
I could.

Left of the Dial

If there's a heaven for me
then it's a place where I'll own
my own radio station.
There won't be many rules.
Basically, people will be able
to play whatever they want
whenever they want.
However, there will be one
inviolable rule: no one can play
any song that sucks – not even once.
And if such a day were to arrive
where a song that sucked was played,
accidentally or not, and I was made aware of it,
I would fire the whole staff immediately — with
full severance pay — then
dynamite the station flat
and let the tower
fall to rust.

Fader Knob

My whole life
it was this way:
when everyone was
listening,
I tended to tune out.
And when no one
was listening,
I tended to tune in.
Now,
someone
could probably
explain
just why that was,
but I promise you,
when they did,
I would not
be listening.

A Parting of Ways (aka Who Made Who?)

I dreamt I was onstage with a guitar,
strumming out some Beatles tunes.
The crowd was sort of into it.
Still drinking their drinks, but not bored.
I looked down into the front row
and Lynyrd Skynyrd himself
was sitting there.
He said, *'Play some Skynyrd.'*
I tried to ignore him,
but he said it again, louder.
'Lynyrd,' I hissed, under my breath,
'come on, man, this is crazy!'
He just looked me in the eye
and said it one more time:
'Play some Skynyrd.'
And right then I knew I could do that.
So I stepped back
and played the bitchin'-est
version of "Free Bird" anybody
would ever care to hear.
It lasted, like, 16 minutes, at least.
I really let it fly on the solos.
The crowd went nuts.
I took a whole bunch of bows.
Lynyrd Skynyrd just sat there smiling.
After the show, he was backstage
waiting for me, like I knew he would be.
I gave him a nod and said,
'Thank you, Lynyrd Skynyrd.'
He shook my hand and said,
'No. Thank YOU, Lynyrd Skynyrd.'
Then he just turned and walked away.
When he got to the backstage door,
I said, *'Wait! If I'm Lynyrd Skynyrd . . .*
who are you?'

He smiled and said, *'I think you know.'*
With that, he pulled out a stick of beef jerky,
took a bite and slipped quietly out into the night.
I stood there alone in the hallway.
Finally, uncertainly, I said,
'Jethro Tull?'

"No one knows you even when you're gone.."
— Freedy Johnston, "This Perfect World"

Curriculum Vitae

Henry Rifle lived on Planet Dust,
beneath a moon,
where everything is dust
and if it's not
it will be soon.

You Had a Busy Day Today

    I think life is a lot like
    any one of those days where you
    find yourself running around like crazy,
    you work your fool tail off
    — nothing seems to go right —
    and all you really want to do is get home.
    And then when you finally get there
    and empty out your pockets, you find
    a Jolly Rancher you'd forgotten about.
    You unwrap it, pop it into your mouth
    and think,
    'Maybe it wasn't such a bad day after all.'

"There's sadness here, a poignancy born of a world where hope is routinely demolished."
            — from "Mr. Mike: The Life and Work of Michael
                  O'Donoghue."

Things Henry Rifle said when he was alive:

"I think if F. Scott Fitzgerald got to know me, really know me — the real me — we would be best friends."

"My advice? Always be yourself. And if that doesn't work, be someone else."

"Would I wrestle Ernest Hemingway . . ? Best of three falls? Yeah, let's do this thing. Let's do it right now!"

"I would never give a trout a cigarette — never. No way, man. That's not my scene."

"I like my clouds smoky — like bacon."

Thanks to Amy and Will —
and Bob and Emily.
Oh, and Blake
and everyone else.

No animals were harmed* during the creation of this book

*Except a whale (minor injuries) — and a wildebeest (deceased).

www.ingramcontent.com/pod-product-compliance
Lightning Source LLC
Chambersburg PA
CBHW021154080526
44588CB00008B/340